EASY

EASY

p o e m s

Roland Flint

*For Artis & John
with fondest memories —*

*Roland
4-99*

Louisiana State University Press

Baton Rouge

1999

Designer: Amanda McDonald Scallan
Typeface: Bembo
Typesetter: Coghill Composition
Printer and binder: Edwards Brothers, Inc.

Library of Congress Cataloging-in-Publication Data

Flint, Roland.
   Easy : poems / Roland Flint.
    p. cm.
   ISBN 0-8071-2261-0 (cloth : alk. paper)—ISBN 0-8071-2262-9 (pbk.: alk. paper)
   I. Title.
  PS3556.L56E18   1999
  811'.54—dc21
                                           98-44085
                                           CIP

The author gratefully acknowledges that some of these poems have appeared before, as indicated below: *After the Storm: Poems on the Persian Gulf War* (Maisonneuve Press, 1992), "Seasonal"; *Colorado Review*, "Grief November" and "Park River Memento"; *Folio/A Literary Journal*, "Ah Venus," "Braid," and "2–26–91"; *Gettysburg Review*, "In a Charles Simic Poem"; *New Virginia Review*, "A Garden in Sicily," "Do You Have an Extra Saw?" and "*Henry & June* the Movie"; *North Dakota Quarterly*, "First Poem" and "Writing Italian Easter (at 'The Foreigner's Desk')"; *North Stone Review*, "The Etruscans," "Flower," "When I Invented the Rose," and "William Stafford's Last Day"; *Painted Hills Review*, "Married"; *Plum Review*, "Easy" and "Pruning"; *Potomac Review*, "Love Story," "Take the Moment: Thursday Aubade," and "Windfall for Edna Millay"; *Southern Review*, "Austere," "HaHa," "Land of Cotton," "Little Men Who Come Blindly," "Singapore," "Strawberries like Raspberries," "Near Arvilla, North Dakota: 1941" and "Never Again Would Birdsong"; and *WPFWFM: Poetry Anthology*, "P & C."
"Prayer" appeared as a souvenir broadside prepared by the Johns Hopkins University Office of Design and Publications to commemorate the author's inaugural as Poet Laureate of Maryland on September 27, 1995. "Monkey House," "After the Spanish Mass with Nena," and "Tom" appeared in souvenir broadsides published by North Carolina Wesleyan College Press.
The author owes a debt of gratitude to Yaddo, where this book found its first shape, and to the Rockefeller Foundation's Bellagio Study and Conference Center, where it was finished.

The paper in this book meets the guidelines for permanence and durability of the Committee on Production Guidelines for Book Longevity of the Council on Library Resources. ♾
This publication is supported in part by a grant from the National Endowment for the Arts.

Easy, easy, I ask you, easy. . . .
Quintus Horatius Flaccus, my good father,
You were just the beginning, you quick and lonely
Metrical crystals of February.
It is just snow.

—James Wright

For Rosalind

Contents

I

When I was eight or nine, Mr. Bina
Showed me how to saw a six-shooter
Out of plywood, which I did. And when
He looked it over, he said it was fine.

One morning when it was gone, and my
Siblings were cleared, mother said:
Honey, your dad kindled the heater
With it, but he didn't understand.

In his Saturday woodcraft classes,
During the war, to tall John Bina
We were equally poets, who taught us
To make ducks, guns, or dowels from wood.

His high Czech face smiled seriously
When he explained: If I'm too old already
For war, I can still teach you about
The woods and saws, mm-hmm, that's good.

No—it wasn't a poem, I'm not sure
It was a pistol, but something
I believed was good. The war and
Woodwork classes ended when I was ten.

Then Clair Clemetson and Bobby Erickson
Came home from the Pacific, at last,
But many from Park River, like
John Kelner and Jimmy Colwell, didn't.

Jimmy's parents still came to the
Lyric Theater, sat halfway back,
Holding hands—and you could hear
Ed's handsome laugh, sometimes.

Not the Kelners: John had been tough
Enough to survive the Bataan
Death March. But then something
Killed him—and sent death home.

3

I didn't know the Binas as a couple,
Blanche and John, except their working
The garden between our houses, and that
Old country delight in their daughters.

Forty-five years later, all five, Irene,
Lorraine, Dorothy, Catherine, and JoAnne,
Were back in town and harmonized—
Full-voiced impromptu singing—at Irene's.

When they got ready to sing in Czech,
The second youngest, Catherine,
Nicknamed Mickey, said, O, I'll cry,
I'm crying already. And they laughed.

The daughters of Blanche and John stood
Singing them back to us, like poets,
No one needing to solo, or shine,
As the best ones rarely do. And it was good.

It is early morning
in Il Giardino Piccolo,
the little garden,
before the best hotel in town,
and a Gypsy mother canters there,
begging quick along the walks.

She thrusts one hand to everyone,
weeping (almost) for the tight-wrapped
bundle, resting lightly on the other arm,
with whom she palms the square,
"Per il bambino, bambino": shill-baby
or doll or rags, wrapped so.

She is wrapped tightly too,
compact as a shetland,
for pitching whatever else
she has, the flat eyes, dull
clothes and skin and teeth,
of poverty—and craft.

Her daughter and partner
of five or six, trails
idly barefoot after, flinging
birds to piquant flight,
as her small hand
fidgets a flowering hedge.

It leads her to an oak,
the upper roots exposed behind
a guard-rail, thinner than she is:
she steps up onto this—and slides
easily along, humming, smiling,
balancing the nonchalance.

In half an hour we'll see her
in the church of Santa Rita,
her set face making believable

the grief of daily begging,
while hungrily hitting
supplicants where they pray.

Her palm she'll offer more like
Madonna than her mother—*Per favore!*
But in this recess she jumps down,
and runs to a marble fountain
at the center of the square,
where she pulls half her body up,

over its marble lip, her pink toes
flexing the air, then pushes off,
sideways—the quick arm-tendons strung—
just far enough so she can slip her
bill into the stream, for this,
her taste of the garden.

For a while, the 3-year-old twins seem as interested as their father, but the 5-year-old keeps tugging his hand. They've been looking at the black rhinos, and the father, leaning and squat, is absorbed in watching a lithe male trying to mount a big, thick cow, who faces a carousel of hay, contentedly chewing.

Heavy rains have left the ground a muddy gumbo wherever the rhinos have made paths, as, especially, all around the carousel. Twice in a row, the dignified cow oblivious, the bull has cranked his hooves and the horny anvil of his head up onto her back.

The exposed, pink—and surprisingly pointed—tip of his eagerness has been an inch from entering when his hind hooves begin to sink in the mud, and he slides back down.

After the second time, all three children are whining, "Let's *go*, Daddy, let's *go!*"

Although the morning is cool, the man's face is hotly flushed: "Just a *minute*," he explains, "*wait!*"

A third time the bull rises up, until, millimeters from paydirt, his back legs trembling, the pointy hind-hooves slowly sink, and down he falls again.

This time he pivots sharply and trots away, then stops short, tenses, and voids—with *great force*—two rectangular turds in a row, like little hay-bales, slap against the mud—*Whap! Whap!*

In *this*, the children are *interested*.

They shout, "*Wow!*"—and "*Whap! Whap!*" and point, and make delighted rillings of laughter. The father, looking down as if wakened, also begins to laugh—and they stroll away towards the monkey house.

Writing Italian Easter

(at "The Foreigner's Desk")

There it is again:
So he is facing east,
The sunrise on his hand.

At the window he sees
It fills the whole horizon—
Red as the risen Christ—

And bright as it shone,
Through crucified glass, into
St. Peter's Episcopal

On an altar boy
Who loved God so
He had to sin away

A call to be His priest,
So not to dirty such
Linens of altar snow.

Now the light moves in a tree,
Which makes, through leafless
Creches and bitten twigs,

A thorn of cross and broken
Thistles, moving to him down
La scrivania dello straniero.

Well, mother, tomorrow night
I will be born, if this were 57
years ago, and you were 29.
Twenty-nine! How young you
would be to me now, mother!
A girl. Were you still
a girl at 29?—having your
fourth baby, your first after
the miscarriage, me?
If I'm thinking of you more,
am I getting ready to be born
again or do I miss you
from reading Juan Rulfo,
who lets the dead
son and mother talk
the way we did so long,
a month before you died,
seven years, 5 months
and 8 days ago, almost 50
years after that night
we beat the doctor
by 25 minutes or so.
Remember? I don't, but
you remembered it to me.
Now I remember to you,
everything, the 40 watt bulb,
the winter, your holding me
aside till the doctor
came to cut the cord.

Little Men Who Come Blindly

Here is my neighbor, a young man,
Out in the street with his son,
Who is about 6, and has his
First bicycle. Like this, Dad,
He says and his father says, no—
Get on like this. Like this, Dad?
Asks the boy, and his father says,

No—like this—when we take the
Training wheels off, you'll fall if you
Get on like that. The boy is
On the bike now and says, like this,
Dad? No, says his father, sit
Back more—re*lax!* Like this? No—no!
And so it goes till they are

Out of my hearing at last. I
Resume cutting the grass, with
Something else making an echo:
How the boy's heart ratchets in
His voice, and I pray I never
Broke from my children's voices
A hurt unfixable as that.

And, while its hasping echoes,
I think of a fine novelist,
In whose teaching the precise
Negatives, word by mincing word,
Paralyze student writers.
Not seeing any connection,
He tells us how his parents,

And especially his father,
Never approved of any
Thing he did, as long as they lived.
He knows that it literally,

And then otherwise, crippled him.
That it took years, a war, and
Stories—his talent—to save him.

And there was my old student,
Who works with the urban poor,
Bringing us his adopted son,
A blackhaired boy named Thomas,
Whom he rebuked harshly in front
Of us, and who said, when our
Friend stepped out, My dad don't like me.

What can we tell the fathers?
And what shall I do with how this
Sounds in me—if writing it
Down isn't enough? What can I
Say to the writer, so he
Forgives his father's hurt enough
To trust his students' failures?

To see them and see himself?
What can I say to my neighbor,
Young enough to be my son?
Some healing words to change him,
Without offense, to help him and
Help his son? *Nothing.* So I tell
You. Is it any use to you?

II

Austere

What did I know, what did I know . . .
Of love's austere and lonely offices?
                            —Robert Hayden

How she left kettles of water
On the kitchen stove for baths
Each Saturday night till hotter
Than needed (add cold), to wash,

In the corrugated tub,
The week's field dirt away,
Blown even into the crib
From a North Dakota sky,

As all of us take turns,
The young mother renewing
Clean heat for each till it runs
Out, as she's finishing hers.

I offer you her kettles, stove,
The kerosene-lamp light,
Her palm her soap her olive,
The tub, its velvety silt.

Near Arvilla, North Dakota: 1941

You go with Grandma to McSharys' farm,
where, in her mid-sixties, she works as cook,
housekeeper, servant—and your local parent.
Avid for the farm, you were generally obedient,
but especially drawn to the bull-pen,
because she'd scared you about its danger,
or for a mystery between the bull and you,
his nostrils snorting you on, the horns
where they rasped a name, his male
fat sack asway with jewels you could fix,
could you just whack it with a bat, Grandma
terrified at the window, too late, you dreamed,
to stop you. And while he groomed his horns
or chewed or splashily peed, the dream went on,
he seeing but ignoring you, a great pitcher
with a pesky runner on first, a few feet
off the bag, testing the bottom strand.

Grief November

Last night the dream of angers
felt like release, like revenge
on all the grieving of the season:
the old ones, mother and son, now
the brother under cancer's blade,
Tom's dead, Nena goes in black—
so yelling at a cop felt right.
Stuart Eisenberg, driving not his
new car but a little white VW,
knocks down a white divider in
the parking lot and, unaware,
begins to drive away, whereupon
a young policeman, enraged and
yelling, runs after him, gun out,
and then begins to *shoot*, for God's
sake, and, without fear, it feels
right to run up to him and start
yelling back, what the hell is he
doing, shooting in such a case,
for Christ's sake, this is traffic,
a minor mishap, an *accident*.
Now Stuart has come back, shaken,
sheepish, but still the rant goes
on, the cop looks scared, he's
green, a rookie, and it feels
therapeutic, if not quite good,
to bully, a little beyond the need,
one green policeman of mischance.

Remember Allen Tate:
who played "Dixie" for us
on his record player, in
Minneapolis, a symphony
orchestra's version,
magisterial Tate conducting,
spiffy and small, with
great arm sweeps and a Jim
Beamishly happy grin
at every *"AWAY AWAY"*—
and who set me up once so:
describing in greater detail
than I remember how he and friends
made gin at home, how they
stole the medical alcohol,
added juniper berries,
or essence of juniper,
some other flavorings
or catalysts I've forgotten
(everything savored in the word
by jubilantly playful Tate),
and put it, at last, into a large
ceramic crock, with a thick
ceramic lid, and left it—now his
aristocratic Southern voice
is back, its British times
Tidewater delicacy, its
handsome male vibrato—
"And then we left it to age,"
the "a" of age held on to,
sonorous and drifting south,
as if leaving both the gin and
tale to age a long, long time.
And who but I the Yankee
straight man stepping right into
the pause with, *"How* long?"
As quickly Tate came back,
with a snapper's grin, "Ah—
about twenty-five minutes."

Tom

The spring goes on without you,
bright squibbing of forsythia
set off by crocuses a week before,
and now, after the tulip tree
and petals from a Japanese cherry,
we have azaleas, ground-tulips,
coarsely delicate primrose, with
pansies, creeping phlox and weeds—
as well as maple, apple, red and
white dogwood—blossoms everywhere.
The spring goes on without you in
your first April dead, and so I
think of it, as it was your first
Thanksgiving not coming to bone
our bird, the first Christmas
without your music and deep
if complicated cheer, the first
Easter, the first Redskins' draft
and the young baseball season,
all which I record for you too.
If the colors of spring are no
brighter, as to Williams's widow,
they are no less bright, or fine
to me, despite my sorrowing,
seeing them, you are gone.

William Stafford's Last Day

Up early to jog and write, alert
For what might show—such as
An Apache word for love, new dirt
On the mole, a snowy pass.

So careful and youthfully fit,
We said he's a cinch for ninety:
He'd have been amused by that,
Knowing: any time is plenty.

His poem was done, when Dorothy
Called and he went to help her. So,
If too soon for us, it was a worthy
Moment for his heart to go.

For whatever epic after that,
He was readier than we, no doubt.

After the Spanish Mass with Nena

On a perfect sunny day,
the temperature not yet up
to its daylong high of 83,
all the neighborhood astir,
with flowers, people pottering,
with greens, breezes, birds,
you think of Tom and feel
peacefully closer to him
or death or eternity or all
the recent not-so-recent dead,
and wonder: why this sense of
a thinning, as it feels to be,
of that distance, as if such
weather is transitional,
as if nearer the other side,
the griefless climates hereafter.
Yes—today, instead of your
tender vexation Tom can't
feel and see and hear
the spring, you think
and pray and almost believe
this is weather to where he is.

III

Take the Moment: Thursday Aubade

Outside our window in Perugia,
a few minutes ago, someone whistled
a song, Neopolitan I think, "O Sole
Mio," anyway in English the one
about there being no tomorrow
so kiss me tonight. Because of
the other noises banging from
the street, I imagine he is one
of the workmen, maybe the same
one who later is riding a jack-
hammer. He's a pretty good
whistler, and lingers with
sentiment over, "so kiss me—
and *hooold* me tight." He even
tries the warble on "just,"
in "there's *ju-u-ust* tonight."
Here's hoping he's no Cassandra
of the hammer: maybe we could
do without tomorrow, but Saturday
we hope to rent a car and drive
to Assisi or San Gimignano.
If so, we will wake next on
the eighteenth anniversary of our
meeting (after Saturday night),
which then would *be* tomorrow,
so kiss me and hold me tight.

Never Again Would Birdsong

A pretty girl writes in her journal
she probably shouldn't put this here,
but she's just had the best sex, *ever,*
in her life, fresh as twenty-two,
says she's had her first orgasm
during intercourse, that they both
came, *at the same time!* that she
finally sees what all the fuss
is about, how this guy is also *fun,*
the laughing they do before and after!—
how it may not—probably won't—last,
but what the hell, it's *so* good now.
And you resist jotting her your theory,
that laughter and orgasm are connected:
those who have a lot of one are likelier
than most to have a lot of the other.
But she must know this in her skin:
we love to make who make us laugh,
even before we feel them one—
come funny honey bone funny come

Braid

After his years of a chronic back,
a chiropractic named Lucy,
with a long dark braid he wants,
advises that when he sits, to put
a quarter inch of newspaper or
magazine down first, under
his buttock on the achey side:
a shim to rolf a little the rack
and pinions of a quirking frame.
This, along with some face down
arm and leg lifts (which suggest
a crab trying to wrong itself),
seems to work: two days now, no
bad news from the southern back.
He feels (for once) well hung—
like her talismanic braid, which falls
straight down when she is still,
but usually is asway, and touches him,
sometimes, as Lucy moves his spine.

Love Story

When the most charming man in Bulgaria
Has butchered, cooked, and fed his pig
Nadia to thirty close friends—Nadia,
Whom he adored but could no longer

Keep in the grains to which she had
Become accustomed—you know things
In the new socio-capitalist economy
Are too hard: beautiful two hundred

Fifty pounds of bristle-white, 10-inch
Snout, hungry, offended, and amorously
Squealing her lover Plamen to fetch
The slops and corn of his troth.

Bless Plamen and forgive him, Lord,
Who tried to be a good pig-priest:
With friends to spill the wine and blood,
To burn Your portion, pray and baste.

Ah, Venus

At the interestingly boring
movie about an opera in Paris,
Glenn Close is aging, but still
she moves you, if not to tears,
with her ability to make them,
real ones, on cue, the camera
full-face on hers as she pumps
them out for the High Hungarian,
he her Maestro, she his Diva—
Big Baton and Bigger Bird—
Who Leave No Tone Unstirred.

Married

On either side of the bed
there is a lamp and hers
she turns sleepily on
when she takes her midnight
walk to the bathroom,
but tonight he's sleepless
and reading late, so,
after gazing about,
she takes her walk
in his light, and
when she comes back,
he sees she's going
to switch hers on,
drowsily thinking off,
and he's moved to turn his
off just as hers flicks on,
the sleepy dear,
who patiently reaches again
to turn hers off and he
times it to turn his
back on just then.
They do this three times,
he laughing silently,
till he leaves it off
at last and sleeps.
She remembers nothing
in the morning
when he tells her,
but she laughs too
and says You're
a wicked man.

Pamela

Praise for Pamela Helen Flint,
who, when Rick's mother called
to say her son was dying,
left at once, expensively, to
fly from Virginia to California
to see him and, as it turned out,
to be the only one with him
when he died: of AIDS, at 27.
Went because she's loved him
since they were fourteen,
maybe before either knew
the complicated calls of sex,
specific measures of need
or predilection, but went on,
as each had promised each,
in love for life. And so just
left school and job and kin,
catching the first flight out,
rented a car in Fresno, drove
fifty miles to the hospital,
to be with him so he knew it:
a wordless surge of greeting
at her voice, crying, and touch.
May all who need one at the end
have such a friend. Praise her.

Easy

While she starts the water and measures the pasta,
he sets the table and peels the garlic.
She cuts up broccoli, strips snow peas, readies fish—
he presses the garlic, fixes her a kir, and him a gin.
She sautés the vegetables while he grates cheese,
readies the candles, and puts flowers on the table.
She puts pasta in the boiling water, and fixes salad,
which he takes to the table with the cheese.
She mixes a salad dressing, he opens the wine
and takes it to the table, where everything is ready,
except for the pasta, so he lights the candles
and puts salad from a big walnut bowl into small ones.

Now she or he brings the pasta, greens and fish
mixed in, and they sit to talk, drink wine and eat.
Though October, they sit on a small screen porch
in the back of the house where they have lived
for twelve years of their twenty together,
the last six, the children gone, alone.
Once, during dinner, if they stop talking
and listen to the music, they may, without drama,
hold hands a moment, almost like a handshake
by now, most friendly, confirming the contract,
and more. She is a pretty woman of 51, who has
kept herself trim and fit. He is 56 and hasn't.

Later, they will clear the dishes and clean up,
and she will bring tea and fresh fruit to bed,
where they will watch a little television or not,
with herbal tea and the fruit. After that, if
they make love or not, they will talk a long time,
her work or his, the budget, the Middle East,
this child or that, how good dinner was, how
easy it is, the times like this, when it's simple.

IV

Windfall from Edna Millay

He didn't know what a windfall was
until he saw one, a circle of apples,
making a collar around its tree,
a couple of apples deep. It was at Millay
Colony, the day before Thanksgiving,
all the trees bare of leaves, even
the one from which they'd fallen
showing only six or so apples
holding out against early winter
and what must have been a bumper
crop. As soon as he saw it he said,
"Windfall, *that's* a windfall," as if
teaching himself a language he almost
knows: from apples what a windfall is.
Of course he wants them to have fallen
all at once, ready as one for the wind,
when it came hard in that direction—
but this is only how strong its figure
is, even facing the literal, as if
the bare field, in which they lay around
the tree, had won the lottery or written,
in one day, a poem of so much apple.

Flower

The crude little rose must be
aluminum, it is so light—
it could be made of rice
or Rice Krispies, gun gray—
a fully opened blossom
is the rose you found lying
in the street and picked up.
Now it blooms from the center
of an International Rotary wheel
you got for bringing poems to men
whose business is to aluminize
anything—even a rose: which is,
sort of, what you did right back,
for a fat fee, at the Rotary lunch,
bootlegging poetry in by limerick,
from innocent suggestives to
the bawdily ambiguous to
a fully aluminized rose.

When I Invented the Rose

It was a kind called red,
because then I knew
only blood-velvets
kissing open like silk,
without a tulip's punning.

Just the licky tip inside,
scents of musk, vanilla,
lavender loams of Kazanluk,
and so subtle you must
put your face in it.

Velvet for the petals,
as I say, or angora.
Thorns?—maybe teased
out by *such* a tongueing
but not in the design.

The backache is nearly gone, thanks
to time and the homosexual masseur,
damned strong and bigger than you are,
whose ads say BODY & SOUL ARE ONE,
and who stretched out the big trunk
muscles to the right of the spine,
from mid-back to under-shoulder,
and every other too, plying lotion
(called *Kiss My Face*), short digits,
forearms, and muscular diligence.
One question lifts its head, as yours
did (well a little) during the hour:
why were you recalling an avid woman
(you never quite had, unless by hand),
as he kneaded about your upper thighs,
bending your knees up to your chest?—
tawny as cream sherry, forty-two,
who moaned along with your bliss,
and rubbed you into her breasts,
saying, Mmm, *this, this* is *it—ooo*,
which is among your sexiest dreams.
Contentedly hetero as you think
you are, what connects these times?
Was it the massage which made Dick,
as Cheever says, put on some weight,
or a fantasy to keep you straight?

She has admired him in print,
his heft and sensual delicacy,
so when she comes to town
they have dinner at his favorite
restaurant, where she insists
on picking up the tab. And they talk:
she knows his words so well, to him
it's another feast, more sumptuous.

On the way back to her hotel,
they stop for brandy, which is
to be his treat, but she pays
when he steps away. Now
they are friends, happily kiting
lines of Roethke back and forth,
laughing, a sound as pleasant
as Courvoisier cognac.

He sees her to her room
to say goodnight and there
he makes a mistake, which
revises their history at once:
her old review, her new one,
a miscue so minute, he thinks,
to one less tuned it might be missed,
in the welter of brandy and words.

But it becomes that meter or two
the Korean navigator was off, which
widens to hundreds of miles,
a lovesong to suspicion:
the missile, a mortal flash
banging dead halfsleeps of hundreds,
a white cold banquet for the sea,
shark and scourer of the small mistake.

Pruning

Here is a letter from an Estonian poet
who wants your stuff for his anthology
of American poems. He is also a physicist,
has a wife and two children, and he says
he's written twice before, giving dates
from seven and four years ago, letters
you never saw. Half the world it seems
is breaking up and those with any
English are fishing for new lives
in the new world—even abject poets
grow hopeful and cast their lines.
An old friend from Bulgaria visits,
another poet, hoping to stay in America,
and, as you walk in the back yard,
he begins to tell you what should be done
to the trees, peach, dogwood, baby
Japanese maple, asks if you have tools.
You fetch a saw and lobber and he sets
to work, with a certainty and speed
which you know is more marketable in
America than any poems. He shows you where
(inside out) and how and how much
to prune and then he does it, you following
with a can of spray for the stubs.
In a little while, in an hour maybe,
all the trees look new, as if they can
breathe again, look healthy—refreshed.
His name is Lyubo and he was born 35 years
ago in a village on the Yugoslav border.
Are such skills a dime a dozen at home?
Or can't his poor garden country use
a poet with a pruning saw just now?
You finish, wash up, and sit together,
where you try to prune the rough English
versions his wife has made of his poems.
He is pleased with your work but you know
that Lyubo in the trees was better.

The wall-eyed waiter is patient
about your wanting the tongue,
which he will bespeak, but why not
first the cabbage salad, finely
chopped with onion and peppers?
(Mix salt, pepper, vinegar, oil.)
With this, maybe slivovits or
sorrel vodka (hold the ice).
The specials tonight: blood
sausage, duck *à l'orange confit,*
and *paella.* As for the wine—
how about the Hungarian red?
It's sweet but doesn't cloy,
and even goes with dessert:
sacher torte, baklava, crème brûlée,
or raspberries fresh as rain.
The floor-show features the
bearded ballerina, a dwarf
contortionist, a philosopher who
yodels, and, at the zither,
a Gypsy who looks like you.
Later, after an espresso, cigar,
and Carlos Uno, you might dance.
With luck, you may be joined by
the ballerina, dwarf, and yodeler,
one in a sleeveless tux—all
tattooed—she with hair *soignée.*

HaHa

If you were milked twice a day and had sex only once a year . . .

You wake up laughing, and try to grab
the gone forever joke in the dream . . . .
Still, you enjoy the laugh as if in
a vacuum and wonder what it is, anyway.

What *is* laughter to cure cancer?
or to surprise a darkness like grief
so that you guiltily clap your mouth?
When Don the bartender said, loudly,
at his boss's funeral, "Hey—a full house—
Bennie would have liked that,"
a few laughed out loud, while
the pews around him prickled.

Why do children, in trouble especially,
feel a dizzy pressure to explode a
haha in the parent, cop, or principal's face?

And why is it cathartic to get into
a laughing jag, the kind that keeps on
rolling, growing, making you cry,
lose breath, lose feeling in your tips
like a mortal symptom?

And this: someone who told you
that after laughing all night,
in the closed bar with its owner,
the owner's wife, and another woman—
all of them full of booze and stories—
laughed so hard he had to lie down,
once, on the carpet next to the booth,
and that after he drove the other
woman home and hugged her, a merely
friendly good-bye hug, he had an orgasm.

So he swore—with no designs on her,
no yearning he was aware of, in the
early morning light, and no erection.
As if sex were jealous of laughter's
horning in—or wanted in on its joke:
to send him home with his messy surprise.
And this: your late friend's late father,
a miscast banker, who used to ask whether
"*Homo sapiens* weighs minutely more or less after
the forcible expulsion of rectal afflatus,"
goofily entertaining the notion that
a buoyancy from unexpended gas might show one
a little lighter, if you had good scales.
How you laughed at the nutty science of that.

(And when you did, were you heavier or lighter
for letting the gas of laughter go?)

So just what *is* it? Something
counter? unmatched? subversive?
Is it metaphysical? metaphorical?
or literal after all? A defeat
for the deconstructionists
and the soul's escape from text—
or a honk at final proof?

Are the rich different from us because
they have fewer laughs, money having stuffed
the cracks which let in spoofs?
No: the laughless are another category
of a soul's homelessness, hunger, and cold,
or, worse, of political rigor.

The word comes partly from "OE *hlowan*,"
not literally to laugh but "to moo,"
and there's its ancient metaphor,
the first poetical farmer saying (in "OE,"
of course) of his laughing enemy or friend,
"What's *he* got to be mooing about?"

So—Why does *the cow have such a long face?*

V

Seasonal, 1991

The last freezing rain of winter
or the first bona fide spring rain
pittering its intermittent music
on the roof and copper gutters
is what you wake to a few days
after the killing has almost
stopped, in the Gulf. It is a sound
filled with cleansing new shingles,
wet and black, with crocuses,
and, just behind them, forsythia,
tulips, azaleas—spring. But it doesn't
wash away last night's news, one
hundred and fifty thousand Iraqis dead,
mostly from our bombing: not
the Elite Guards, but less loyal
Muslims, Kurds, and Christian Assyrians,
driven out to and trapped on
the front lines of policies
for which they did not vote or elect
to die, these weeks black rain fell
down, in light or dark, day in,
night out, a bloody, percussive
anthem to our great victory over
Saddam and the inhuman poor.
Now, while the lisping patter
genially wakens our house in
a birdsung Maryland suburb,
in Baghdad a season of heat and winds
of cholera and typhus begins.

Strawberries like Raspberries

A few years ago in Bulgaria,
in Boyana, outside Sofia,
you had the best pear of your life,
a Bosc, and then another:
they had the highest pear taste,
the chewiest sweetness, an apple's
snap of October, the genius
or luck of Bulgarian horticulture,
which has also given the best
cherries, strawberries, and peaches
of your life. The strawberries were
small, a delicately sweet dark red,
and a friend called them, in Bulgarian,
"strawberries-like-raspberries," which
you misunderstood, taking that to be
a varietal name of *this* strawberry:
that is, "raspberryan strawberries."

And the next day, shopping alone,
you puzzled and amused the grocer,
asking in your baby Bulgarian,
for *yagodi kato malini*, the
"strawberries like raspberries."
In one of your Bulgarian reading
lessons, in the communist textbook,
the country is called a "garden paradise,"
and so it seemed, always, on many visits.
But now you keep hearing and reading
about the brutal shortages of transition,
as if glasnost and apples can't
break from the same blossoms,
as if the national white cheese,
a finer feta, from cows or goats,
as if the velvet yogurt, even milk,
even bread, even your favorite
grape brandy, are failing to find

their mouths: as the old systems
of supply and distribution, or
of politics and privilege, die
by their own dead weight or
from the freedom now to say so.

As if, for a while, at least,
the harvest will be only of fruit—
bitterer than sour cherries—
of what had been more deeply sown.

Park River Memento

The summer I was eighteen I was
Carrying hod for the construction
Of a big new potato warehouse
In Park River: and every morning
Frank Erovik (pronounced *Urvik*) would grin,
Call me Horse, in his gravel mutter,
And ask me, Did you get a little
Last night? 'n' gawdammit tell the truth.

I don't recall if I told the truth
(Which would be no), but sometimes I would
Say: Sure, Frank. And you? how about you?
He'd say, O, I had a yen last night,
But the old lady was turned the other
Way, so I said the hell with it. Once
He growled, By God, I did—this morning—
The alarm clock and me and the old
Lady all went off at the same time!

It was many years later and I
Was gone far from home in my new life,
When I heard how Frank had ended his.
That when stones in his throat had hardened
To cancer there or in his larynx,
And the pain dug in, Frank, big-bellied
And lame, bent over and ran as hard
As he could headfirst against the door
Of a granary or barn (funny?—
But true)—out to snap his neck, I guess.

And tried, after that, it appeared, to
Crack his skull open with a hammer.
(He wanted death, but she'd turned away?)
How, bleeding and numb, he rigged a rope
To a beam, at last, and swung on out.
The next time I saw Frank it was his
Head only, a good sketch Sam Knutson
Had done, in a window at *The Press*,
In pencil, Frank's red face flat and grey.

Stanley Kauffmann doesn't like it,
and, ok, it drags a little,
but there are some moments:
as when Anaïs tells Henry
she's happy they fit so good,
how sometimes she has to
vaseline her husband's Hugo,
and Henry snaps a quarter second
stare that says he too's been taught
the faith of every modest male:
all dicks are roughly the same.
Stan *is* on the money about June,
or the tall invert who plays her,
what a honey furnace she is,
especially with her dampers
down. But if he really means it
when he says the Anaïs isn't sexy,
Stanley needs an oil change,
or lube job, and he'd better get
that tailpipe checked.

Do You Have an Extra Saw?

What a pleasure, to work four hours
in the yard, sawing pine and linden
branches into lengths for the outdoor
barbecue pit. You work and sweat,
non-stop, except for some tea once,
water a few times, and some talk
with Slavi, the intelligent man
who saws the branches off, rebuilds
a section of the stone wall behind
the house, replaces some slates
on the roof, and in minutes stacks
all the wood you've cut and brings you
more. As he is finishing his work,
he notices a stone missing from
the terrace in front of the house,
instantly finds a flat one its size,
and so he digs up the space and
places it expertly on the spot.
Afterward he and you share a beer
with dinner and you think, sitting
outside to eat, in Knyazhevo, on
the porch, that beer has never
tasted better. Generously,
they, your Bulgarian hosts,
mistake you for an intellectual,
and so are somewhat surprised
at your tireless sawing. But you,
of course, are better at this than
at poems, teaching, or at learning,
in late middle or very early old
age, a hard Cyrillic language.
But, in your labors and in your brew,
you speak clear Slavi and he speaks you.

Singapore

The beautiful blossom in Singapore,
In its low sun and tropical rain:
Chinese flowers both women and men,
Malaysians too and dark-skinned Tamils.

Fair or dark, the faces are nectarine,
Hair cleaner than fur in the sun,
Eyes darker than moon-tipped water—
Especially exquisite Tamil girls'.

Seeing no irregularity for weeks,
In the big hotels, in buses, trains,
At the zoo and botanical gardens,
You begin to think it paradise.

Then, at a food booth near downtown,
A Chinese boy, in profile orchid smooth,
Gets up and turns a face that becomes,
From his nose to past the other ear

Half an inch of dry-rot, scabbed
And black, a birth mark's gumbo, hard
And cracked, cross cut by pubic beard,
Coarse itching of buffalo shag: as if

Difference *will* get in, and leave,
From malice held back, more dark,
One nail-tip scratching filthy half
A human face in pretty Singapore.

Etruscans

1. At the Etruscan Well in Perugia

Three or four hundred years before
Christ, the Etruscans dug a hole
at the best confluence of springs,
here in Perugia, and built a well
to last, if not forever, till now:
the centuries have piled on 450
meters or so of the layered busyness
since, so you have to walk down
many steps through an excavation
in order to see its top, under which
are the great central travertine
beams weighing 80 tons apiece
leaning to pinch in place, if
not forever, the central stone, far
above the unstill waters, circled,
up to the beams, by the great walls
of brick-like rock, down which
constantly trickle the abiding
ingenuities of Etruscan water.

2. At the Etruscan Museum in Rome

Besides wells, architecture, and
engineering to move a quarry,
they seem to have been best at
killing, necrotic art, and sex.
As you'd expect from its sound,
elegant, cruel, deft, and smart,
Etruscan. Rectitude, knife-rasp,
forced entry, Etruscan. Arms
long as Giacometti, horse-clop,
empire, deep wells, big stones,
javelins, carriages, Etruscan.
Males, carnage, sex, and death.
Power to move love and terrify.

Prayer

Any day's writing may be the last,
He's reminded at 2 in the morning,
Making this year's last Italian
Notes, before readying his machine
And self to get aboard the bigger
Machine and fly, Dio Volente, *home.*
And so he repeats the Our Father
He said to himself before rising.
And feels a heartfelt thanks, Lord,
For such poems as have come his way,
Whether or not they get read, and,
It goes without saying, few may.
And thanks as well for eagerness,
Almost daily, to greet the drone
With words, bequeathed in part
By what poets before have done:
He prays to be among them, one,
However small. The work is all.